RED HILL

❖

PETER BRANSON

SELECTED POEMS

2000-2012

Belfast
LAPWING

First Published by Lapwing Publications
c/o 1, Ballysillan Drive
Belfast BT14 8HQ
lapwing.poetry@ntlworld.com
http://www.freewebs.com/lapwingpoetry/

Copyright © Peter Branson 2013

Since before 1632
The Greig sept of the MacGregor Clan
Has been printing and binding books

All Lapwing Publications are
Hand-printed and Hand-bound in Belfast
Set in Aldine 721 BT at the Winepress

ISBN 978-1-909252-37-0

ACKNOWLEDGEMENTS

Poems in this selection have first appeared in the following
poetry magazines, anthologies and literary periodicals:

Acumen, Agenda, Ambit, Anon, Envoi, The London Magazine,
The Warwick Review, Iota, The Frogmore Papers, Fire,
The Interpreter's House, Other Poetry, Poetry Nottingham,
The Recusant, South, The New Writer, Crannog,
The Columbia Review, The English Chicago Review,
The Huston Poetry Review, Barnwood, The Able Muse,
Indigo Rising, Fuselit, Bravado, Westward Quarterly,
Starlight, The Morning Star, The Hot Air Quarterly, Ardent,
New Leaf, The Coffee House, Blinking Cursor,
Journeys Through Fire, The Stony Thursday Book,
Emergency Verse, The Robin Hood Book, Night Balancing,
Raw Edge, Not Only the Dark, Spillway, Sarasvati,
Monkey Kettle, De La Mancha, Off the Coast.

CONTENTS

NANNYGOAT LANE 7

ATTILA THE NUN 8

JUBILEE 9

THE BIG GAME 10

THE SALVAGER 11

TIME TRAVELLING 12

THE BLOOD EAGLE 13

GOBBY 14

ICE MAIDEN 15

HOLY JOE'S 15

WITH THE FAIRIES 16

SANDPIPERS 17

JENKIE 18

ROOK PIE 18

MOVING DAY 19

BENEATH RED HILL 21

FIRST SIGNS 22

ROCKY ROAD FROM DUBLIN 23

MEN'S WORK 24

ON THE OLD BOG ROAD 25

AT THE RISING OF THE MOON 26

HEROES 27

GEORGE GREEN 28

THE TIME THE LIGHT WENT OUT 29

STILL LIFE WITH FLOWERS 31

GHOSTS 32

WHATEVER HAPPENED TO WILLIAM? 33

ONE FOR SORROW 35

POEMS 'N' PINTS 36

SIXTIES 37

MARRIAGE LINES 38

E EQUALS M C SQUARED 39

LIFE CLASS 40

THE BARTHOMLEY MASSACRE 41

KITE FLYING 41

ENDGAMES 42

'HIGH HO SILVER, AWAY!' 43

SHADOW DANCERS 45

THE CURLEW 46

'RAINDROPS KEEP FALLING ON MY HEAD' . 47

"SOME BLESSED HOPE" 48

COMIC CUTS BIN LADEN 49

THE BOAT HOUSE 50

FOUND 51

CROW BAIT 52

ONE STEP AWAY 53

THE BIG PICTURE 53

RED STREET 54

RETROSPECT 54

THE FLAX BOW 55

MUMMY'S BOY 55

RODE PARK 56

SPIN 56

BALLAD OF STEPHEN LAWRENCE 57

THE CLASS WAR 58

DOG SOLDIERS 59

THE HADITHA MASSACRE 60

HILLSBOROUGH 62

PUB FOLK 64

KINDOKI 64

FOX TOR MIRES 65

NARROW-BOATS AT RODE HEATH RISE . . . 65

FOLK RISING 66

'JUST YOU WAIT AND SEE' 67

SCOUSE JACK 68

MISE-EN-SCÈNE 69

MARILYN 72

ESSERE AMATA AMANDO 72

THE SPIRIT MASK 73

NANNYGOAT LANE

Pressed underneath the bank,
wrapped round the text
of an old willow stump
you found the fox,
mealy and mangled
as a beached fur coat
ironed out into
the eager leeching silt.

Two centuries
of fabricated flow
par-filled and dried
that pool above the mill:
one sultry afternoon
whole race broke ranks,
its destiny revised
inside a cloud.

Site where you swam,
scaled heights, acted in dreams -
reel upon reel,
watched floats bitten with hope,
frst, weeds and grasses
whispered, willow sprouts
now roar out thirty feet
above the ground.

Safe on the shoulders
of your grandfather
tied in by huge bear paws,
tall as the clouds,
you scoured the wooded tracks
for unicorns
with finest ivory
proud on their brows.

ATTILA THE NUN
For Mo

Tag she gets lumbered with,
but only in bad dreams
and never to her face.
Trade name is Sister John
the Baptist. Bit on view,
from lower brow to chin,
looks early twentyish.

Her skin is palest pink,
translucent, viewed against
the stark, starch, habit-white,
black-shrouded penguin suit.
Dominican brand rite:
no soiled grey in betweens;
evil and good, dark – light.

Nails perfect sheening health,
eyes gleam like sculpted ice,
frigid, inflexible,
stern as a ruler's edge,
strict as a Mackintosh
upright, drives sin from kids,
scourges and terrifies.

Children who come to her
suffer, sweet Jesus knows,
except the day you spy
her with an angel (five
years old found crying on
the yard) proud on her knee:
"So beautiful," she sighs.

JUBILEE
"Jack be nimble,
Jack be quick,
Jack jump over
The candlestick" (anon.).
For Brian Lythgoe

Day she gets crowned, you hardly see a thing,
at worship round that eight-inch gogglebox,
Rosarean Club, with half the parish wrapt,
like sympathetic string. As rare back there
as outhouse loos today and rationed, wire-
less king, ghosts float before your eyes, reflect
grey-flannel world outside. Mind set one mean-
street, ranger ride away, sneak home to build
an outlaw roost behind the chicken coop.
You're down four foot before you know, see off
light rain with hessian and cane, off-cut
broadloom for floor, snug as a grave. You swot
star-spangled comic book, Jumping-Jack-Flash
in mask, republican, suck sweets and dream.

THE BIG GAME

Teams chosen, them or us, mealtimes by passed,
errands forgot; no room for arguments,
no referee, twin banks of brotherhood.
To win's the thing and yet no lines are crossed.
Coat goals, width handicap, dependent on
the goalie's size and score, no other rules,
nor gaps the devil can squeeze through, the stir
of sex red-carded, growing up postponed.
A puppy on eternal string, play ebbs
and flows. On borrowed time, you're drawn towards
street light, parental anger stewed, the clock
ignored. Nothing can match the joy, each feel
of foot on ball. What's more, deep down you know
to stop will break the charm, perhaps for good.

THE SALVAGER

He spent his hard-earned freedom in this shed,
two bar electric fire, appraising form
and filling betting slips, old woodwork tools
and garden implements fussed over, rubbed
to sheen with oily rag, at our expense.
No doubt he was at home here making stuff,
his fag end glowing on/off, like Morse code.
The smell's what kicks you when you first come in,
that mix of sawdust, polish, oil and damp.
His workbench fills one end and there are shelves
on all four walls, with jam-jars full of strange
concoctions, tins of every shape and hue,
unlabelled so you've no idea what lies
within, yet he knew perfectly each one:
drill bits, nuts, bolts, nails, screws, rawl plugs and such,
then underneath, in ordered piles, used wood.
For nothing went to waste; spent happy hours
recycling stuff. He'd tease out nails from planks,
tap-hammer them till straight - against his vice.
He fashioned things with craft and care, each joint
perfection, never mind how long it took,
his coat slung on a nail inside the door,
the pockets tired and sagging out of true.
"Man of few words," Macmillan nurse explains
when you turn up just after he has gone.
Later, you howl, pummel the steering wheel.
Hot tears, bleak school reports, cold war missiles,
dark Hindley clones lurk deep inside your dreams.
He sneaks in here when trouble brews: "I'm down
this week," he sighs, short-changing her again.

TIME TRAVELLING
('Muscicapa Striata: The Spotted Flycatcher')

Each year they journeyed north, from Africa
your bird book said; re-laid that cunning nest
in same small cleft in your old garden wall.

Next spring you'd always doubt that they'd come back
those measured boyhood years as you stacked up,
yet every time they did.
                   Inclined, it seems,
to cut things fine, you'd catch them at their ease
long after all your other visitors
had settled in to breed: and so discreet;
such inborn, fragile elegance; ash brown
above a creamy, dappled breast; what taste!

Dash out in twisty, darting flight to snap
up insects on the wing: turn deftly back
to self-same spot they started from, like kids
used to in playground games embracing chalk
and token bits of brick.
                 Eggs warm to touch,
you'd gaze in wonderment; translucent, pale
and delicate, pure porcelain; flecks shades
of gilded bronze, the Midas brush: too soon
that thankless task, striving to pacify
those gaping famished mouths.
                 One day you'd look
and they'd be gone: at first you'd feel bereaved;
but soon enough you'd dream and conjure up
dimensions and strange distances, conceive
exotic latitudes you'd never seen.

Now you've long flown and your old habitat
has been turned down, with six new houses schemed:
that's progress, you concede, fast in the fourth
dimension where your travellers still breed.

Peter Branson

THE BLOOD EAGLE
Thanks to 'The Observer Book of Birds'

You're dressed, first light, before the rest have stirred,
the only one alive on whispering sands,
except some way-off bloke along the bay,
beside his telescope, out with the tide.

"A sea eagle." Asked if you want a look,
you can't say no, make out an upright shape
at least a mile away across the bar.
You know he's right; you've gleaned it from your book.

Same postage-stamp, iconic stance, you say
they've long died out. "A wanderer," he smiles,
"from Scandinavia." The statue stirs;
winged sail, red shepherd sky, dawn sacrifice.

Can't wait to tell them at the boarding house.
Defying gravity, first bouncing bomb
then low-slung Lancaster, you watch it till
there's nothing there to see, time in reverse.

Less anger than relief, strange men a straight
red card, they're on your case. Lips sealed, you sound
silent retreat, trail tears of cupboard grief.
Tongue tied, hot beans to spill, you rage inside.

Horned devils armed with broadsword, axe and spear
spew from the dragon's mouth, as quiet as wraiths.
With famished rabid strides you make high ground
before church bells cry foul, whole town asleep.

GOBBY

Tag you got lumbered with first day; real name
I've no recall. You hardly ever spoke;
gestures with single words attached made do,
but symbols raised you up, 11plus and all.
Bolted, thin as an unstrung bow, all eyes,
you stooped to suit, With Tonka hands and feet,
stilt arms and legs like loose-strung bags of bones,
pure pantomime, it never worked. I joined
your scourging, swallowed pride; when things died down,
played faithless Peter by your side, for you,
pie crust of permanent surprise baked on
your doughy face, were indispensible.
A natural, you'd spy a nesting hole
at thirty yards. With birds, somehow you knew.
Outside your territory you'd point which patch
the garden warbler's nest would be, spot where
the barn owl should appear and she'd be there,
pale as a ghost, gilded and quartering.
You taught me how to crouch low down against
the sun, spot fertile shapes in silhouette.
Unlike most kids, you never took the eggs;
your pockets bulged with pellets, feathers, skulls.

ICE MAIDEN

"Married the job," but at what cost (Mum talk),
way back? Dad's two pints proud: "Inspector in
the Force, retired with cataracts, own house."
Like rusty headlamps on her goggled Sprite,
tight-lipped, not able to relax, knick-knacks
at risk, those frog eyes follow me around.
Thick lenses wither, halos of white light,
garaged, widescreen, gimlet-gaze magnified.

That photograph of her, at home amidst
a band of men, dress uniform, hair in
a bun; one bloke has pinned her medal on,
stout-chap handshake, "Hold it!" smile like the sun.
I ask in vain. No one can tell me what
she's done: "Dark deeds," nod and a wink, "Hush-hush."

HOLY JOE'S

Second-hand uniform, that oafish 'BUZZ'
you fellow-travel on, your shame-faced badge
home-sewn, blunt vowels don't suit, sarcasm wounds.
All smog and mirrors, hell, confess or burn,
they're sworn to mould your rounded nurture till
it fits their set-square rules; get off on it,
three minute warning, strap, Guinness black-white,
low 'Sixties', Christian Brothers' grammar school,
red tram lines, dough-soft palms. Obliged, you strive
at first. It seldom works; incongruent,
no spark inside. Slapped down, turn other cheek,
feral, long hair, mischief personified.
An émigré, first foot in neither camp,
rules bend, swing on the breeze; you muddle through.

WITH THE FAIRIES

"Off with the fairies" mime
his stock response,
next thing you know
she's wandering the streets
the worse for wear,
nudge – wink,
in underclothes.
Well that's the storyboard
they consummate.
What price the matriarch
you call to mind:
wallpaper, curtains, furniture
replaced near spanking new;
a paint brush close to hand
and pot of brilliant white
for touching up
her spotless widowhood?
The son is blunt
with rage: "End of the day
she doesn't know
my bloody name."
Soon she is diagnosed,
concealed from view.
He never visits, come
what may. Alive
or dead, house sold to pay
her dues, she's with
the fairies either way.

Peter Branson

SANDPIPERS

You notice every time you pass, old pub-
sign faded to a pallid afterthought,
like watercolour ravished by the sun.
You've never been inside, imagining
tar-varnished walls, tired furniture, cramped style.
Recall your visitor, aged nine, disturb
him from his meal, pipe-dream, small patch of silt
above the broken wheel and silent mill.
Too small and delicate to be a snipe;
no side-step zig–a–zags to beat retreat,
as though rehearsing hungry sparrow hawk
locked on or two cocked barrels-worth in tow.
You conjure up a likeness in your book,
stir every word to taste; like wine, improves
with age, "The Shadow Of Your Smile" refined
and more intense. Forewarned by piercing three-
note cry, you've scanned the pool for strangers through
tall reeds and sedge, then watched the bobbing head
and tail, those stiff, bowed wings in ticking flight.
You clamber back, through feral dank remains
of ornamental Wilderness, last trace
of fallen country pile, now real estate,
to watch the willow warbler flit from tree
to bush, a loose leaf nervous on the breeze,
until it falls to ground and disappears
beneath low bramble and rough thatch. Can't find
the nest that stares you in the face. Retreat,
like yesteryear, and wait. Return to flush,
x mark the spot, eye focus, magnetise.
Slow fuse, tired synapses explode; inside,
the penny dropped, silk featherbed, six eggs,
translucent orbs of light, pearls frecked with gold.
You hold one in your palm, the urge to take,
as kids do then, impossible to quell.
You prick and blow the yolk; reprise next day,
corpse at the wake, sheen spent, dry brittle shell.

JENKIE

Can't raze it from my brain, that Christmastime
you spewed the claret down on Stafford Street;
worked in between the cobbles, wrinkled, crazed,
all weather face. Drunk as a leaping lord,
knocked from your ninepins by a headstrong car.
Was never caught. He felt your collar though.
"The impact snapped the second vertebra":
that skittled you. An educated man,
quizzed on election night which lot would win;
slow pause into your drink: "The ruling class."
(Your poaching mates stand for your funeral.)
Brief instant and you've nodded out of view,
into the swaddling wind and shrouding rain,
into the knowing dark where you belong.

ROOK PIE
*"Sing a song of sixpence,
a pocket full of rye."* (Trad)

Plump squabs fresh from nest were treats way back.
Told how he scaled, swayed in frail rigging, wing
'n' prayer, green besoms in clenched fists the glue
that bound, singled him out from Icarus.
Graveside, words spent, you view the spire beneath
Red Hill. A beech stand screens old town and new.
See in its topmast reach, ink blemishes,
x rays of bleeds that fetched him here today.
Black birds, our noisy neighbours, nomads from
the Steppes, here centuries before those bells
were cast, are oil-on-water sheen close up,
soft purples, blues and greens, like dragonflies.
They shoal at dusk, like mating galaxies,
cavort and kiss, one consciousness, one will.

Peter Branson

MOVING DAY
For Aunty Win

Before they reached the bridge
she saw the boats,
begged them to stop.

She knew the way the breeze
stirred them to life,
relaxed then taut again
against their mooring rights.
They shoaled small daubs
of light across the wides
like herring schools.

She wrote the message carved
into the slab below
the massive coping stone.
'My age,' she murmured
at the number 68 ...
'We had a boat like that
after the war.'

They started off
back down the telescope's
cruel eye, concealed
behind a bank of cloud;
both hands loud round
the handle of her bag;
white knuckle ride,
that frightened fey
behind the eyes.

'She doesn't know
my bloody name!' he snapped,
so angry with the world
he'd known and her.
'Stop that!' she warned.
'Children who swear
deserve a smack.'

Outside himself, he laughed.
'Perhaps she could have coped?'
his partner asked.
First time they'd found her out
he'd thought her drunk.
Eventually they talked
the doctor round.

'Well this is really nice.
It's ages since
we've been out in the car':
smile of content,
then warned her husband
of the road ahead
and him already
more than ten years dead.

BENEATH RED HILL
In memory of Ed Wright

1.

On holiday, long summer haul, fifteen,
I call on you, tight cobbled space behind
the cinema where Saturdays, aged eight,
from ten-fifteen, I queue for matinees
with mates, clock grainy old B western films.
Blisters my badge of pride, I yearn to be
like you, a working man in your flood prime.
Tarmac and dustcart gangs all take the piss.
I burn brick red. You ride as Tom Mix would.
"Tough sod but fair, Fred Wright," Jack Jenks has said.

2.

That stroke draws all your pride, word-shy, grid-locked
with concentration and embarrassment.
You know about the embolism, tick
on, borrow time - yet never tell your wife.
Talk tunes to old times you relent, restore
now bristling Lichfield Street, *"A mere dirt track
for cart and carriage"* where the nouveaux-riche
with Rolls or Bentley, bottle banks at Stoke,
build villas, ride to hounds, rough-shoot, a short
train ride from enterprise, slum-killing smoke.

3.

Low Anglican among massed Catholics,
a martyr to hard drink, I watch him edge
to your graveside. Their holy water words
well-spread, crumbs rap the coffin, like raised fists
on angry doors. *"Sound bloke, your Uncle Fred."*
Your education life, your geometry
the perfect squaring of a garage base,
you've earned your neighbourly footprint, know how
folks tick; part of your signature, your firm
handshake, the solid ground beneath my feet.

FIRST SIGNS
For George and Len Pickering

"Don't look so worried son."
He hails you through,
ghost bricklayer, propped up
in fire-side chair,
frail, dogged before
his day by dodgy chest.
Familiar faces from
your childhood, aunts
and uncles, neighbours,
slowly penny-drop
you, born and bred
two streets across;
first time you've been
since you moved house at eight,
fresh down from university
to join his wake.

Swearing an oath
of brotherhood
to make ends meet,
pay doctors' bills
pre national health,
seemed sensible way back
to working folk.
High crime to greet
with Oddfellows
two hundred years
ago, en masse,
sisters as well,
panic at Peterloo,
slaughter from France.

Peter Branson

ROCKY ROAD FROM DUBLIN
For Keith, Kathleen, John and Dot

This place has grown a skin
like drying turf; the quaint decay
incensed by snarling traffic fumes
and goosed by all things new.
Rare times revised; seduced
by ancient history, Danelaw
and Eurogeld: 'Queue now
to view the Book of Kells!'

Though folk still cross themselves,
talk tongues like a tridentine rite,
good craic's the wanton whore,
mass genuflection of the will,
mouth music piped and pitched
at tourists tamed and canonised.
Flipside of bright new store some wag
has scrawled: 'I spend therefore I am.'

He hardly breaks the countertop.
Pure leprechaun: *'Ah that boreen,*
so quiet. Sure you could murder him
(sly dig) *no one would know.'*
They think the church has lost its way.
He gestures to the motorbike
outside the presbytery (eye jig):
'A two-stroke priest, yer man. Can't cope.'

High hills, cruel archaeology
raw as a curlew's eye; roadhenge:
echoes of ambulance cast down
some wormhole-callused sky;
'Enough to wake the dead!' – grave goods
to conjure ancient wailing rites,
draw power from what lies beneath,
unction for mating of hurt minds.

The lone turf-cutter harvesting:
he gathers up the half-dried sods,
air drowsing with the reek
of drying peat, his face the tinct
and texture of the turf itself –
couchant, through troubles times
and martyrdoms, like those sealed in
the Seven Sleepers' den.

MEN'S WORK
Wicklow, October 1920

Home from the hills, like wraiths in starless night,
the Boys make tracks, cross old turf working, gorse
and heather moor. Broad daylight, pistols tucked
inside your knickers, you're the gunslinger.
Crude hardness bruising chaste white thigh, each sign-
post one more Station-of-the-Cross, you're bound
for town. Mouth parched, loose talk or treachery
bad news, sweat beads anointing brow and nape
like rosaries, you draw more secular
responses from the Black an' Tans who guard
the bridge. At Mass, the Lads make furtive craic,
like émigrés, outside the high church door.
Such scant observance male preserve, you kneel
within, amenable, head veiled and bowed.

Peter Branson

ON THE OLD BOG ROAD
County Galway, Ireland

His face adds texture to the ground he cuts.
Cured by the wind and rain and written on
like pages from long-faded paperbacks,
he's tenure here. Recall to mind those men
you laboured with, who mocked your eagerness
through smiling eyes, fond summer days on roads
and building sites. The air is dozy with
the sense of drying peat. You watch him turn
new-sheening turves to cook, then try his spine,
lean on his crook to craic the time. "I worked
the motorways for years. This called me back."
He's shaman-wise, stacks visionary truths,
old as these hills, we burn unwittingly,
like youth's fair-mindedness, to smoke and dust.

AT THE RISING OF THE MOON
"And hurrah! me boys, for freedom;
'tis the rising of the moon."
(From 'The Rising of the Moon' by John Keegan Carey)

For Luke Kelly, folk singer: 1940-1984

The awesome present of your voice: outside
the angry guttur of a power saw;
slowly the copper beech across the way
is layered to the floor. The Council say
it's wormed inside and dangerous, mindful
of recent winter storms when branches tore.
Blank arc of sky, I loved that rich red down,
cool stillness of its crown of quiet shade.
Looked worth another hundred years and more
but cankered in the core it had to fall.

Feral red hair, rash beard and navvy looks,
you work each song as though it is your last;
a wild wood-kerne, veins cabling from your neck
as unequivocal as gelignite.
Beneath a rover's weather-battened face
and dancing tongue, you charm tired simple tunes,
breathe text to life transporting minds and souls.
Unglazed by sophistry you clarify
what's right, inspire us with pure energy,
complexity resolved to black and white.

Banjo divining like a Thompson gun,
you cast our doubts and forge an attitude:
raw undirected anger driven straight
inside the heat of things; fuse life and art
in perfect symmetry that's understood.
The heroes you revered died sound, culled long
before their time. This tree, now a mere graze
of dust upon the ground — like you, inside,
the incubus had gorged and thrived; too brief
that span between the two great mysteries.

HEROES
'The pony jerks and the riot's on.'
(From 'Clearances': S. Heaney)

Tromping to Monsalhead and back with friends,
you pause near dank cold Demonsdale beneath
a fitful crowded sky, mapping your mood
where Devil's Scabious turns green banks haze-blue.
Parade of Heroes, the Olympic dream
fulfilled: no lives at risk from those who fight
(Afghanistan, Iraq), or those who don't,
no bones wrong – right; no loving sacrifice.

Take Heaney's great-grandmother, off to Mass
in her new husband's trap for the first time,
mobbed by the Orange gang she'd left behind.
Sense neighbourly outrage, well-hurled insult,
riding the Troubles straight through here and now,
white-knuckled cobbles, blood across the page.

GEORGE GREEN

'What means these ridiculous monstrosities in the court of cloisters?'
(St Bernard of Clairvaux, 1125).
'The symbols are ingrained in the psyche … since the dawn of human existence.' (G. R. Varner).
'The Green Man': term coined by prominent folklorist, Lady Raglan, circa 1939.

Shaped from heart wood, hard stone, no figment, flesh
and blood transformed by low-born artisans,
these fiendishly-depraved eyesores, symbols
employed to decorate high corbel, roof
boss, font, bench-end and startled misericorde,
kept fussy church officials ignorant
of what they represent, the living sap
within the gnarled dark root, those furtive eyes
above old chapel doors, the dancing men
and stag-horns peeping out from altar screens.

"The Reverend Griffith took me to his church,
showed me this curiosity in oak,
with leaves and branches sprouting from the mouth
and ears, entirely smothering the face."
Jack in the Green's abroad. No begging game
by lean black chimney sweeps in garish clothes,
led by a hobby horse; wild kettle drums,
whistles and frying pans, this one's for real.
Where branches arch beyond the grazing height,
you'll find his signature. D'you understand?

Those haunted eyes, gaunt cheeks and knotting brows:
there's something present here we've never known
yet recognise, an energy, a fugue,
the spirit present in each cell of plants
we eat, flowers we smell, the air we breathe.
These days George Green's despondent, gaunt, afraid
he lacks the strength and cunning to redeem,
restore our baneful toxic fingerprint;
no breathing space to beat retreat, for seed
to relocate, mature, habituate.

THE TIME THE LIGHT WENT OUT

How did the Dark Age come?

                        The power wound down.
There'd been some temporary rationings
but this time they'd been warned it was for good.
Cookers lay barren, central heating stalled
and kettles lacked the will to mash the tea;
no candles left to burn, light chased the sun.
Lids flipped, big-time; weird portents, false sunsets.
The web and mobile culled, churches swelled up -
'All day confessionals.' They soon got used
to life without TV; had radio,
just BBC and certain hours per day:
'Don't panic. It will do more harm than good.'

Then what?

                  Home freezers stank. Cards idle, cash
points blunt - rioting: *'All looters will be shot!'*
Shops glass-eyed blanks and supermarket shelves
exposed, how people change ... They hid what food
they'd got. Pet cats and dogs soon disappeared.
Gunfire was circumspect, mostly at night:
can't live on love. Tap water was unsound;
rubbish and sewage stacked. With pharmacies
racked dry, they dropped like pins: Death rock 'n' rolled.
The mood turned desperate: a boy was birched
for stealing cabbage leaves; black marketeers
and deviants were scourged and strung from trees.

Who lived and died?

> Folk tried to flee the towns
and cities. All known exits batten-downed
and booby-trapped, a few got out on foot
before the walls of razor wire went up.
From then escape well nigh impossible,
Badlands we shun today, rank with hindsight,
became death camps. Nine out of ten expired:
many gave up the ghost. But where we are,
farm stuff long commandeered, some held their breath:
with notice of old ways you kept alive.
Gamekeeper, poacher, new age traveller
survived The Cleansings; gypsies dined like kings.

STILL LIFE WITH FLOWERS
For Elizabeth Constance

Day of your funeral
was rainbow grey.
Though you have gone
it hasn't stalled the rain.

Chromosome 22:
no wassail song,
nil chance to thrive,
to toast the apple man
in constant rhyme;
*"Dire quality of life,
twelve months at best"*.

I signed the paper, stilled
your faint footprint,
then bore you blitzed with love,
dumb as a stone;
baneful inheritance,
bite-size, conceived too late.

Lukewarm, I hold
you like a photograph.
That cold churchyard;
next door a whistle blew.
The school cried foul,
skipped beats of perfect time:
 "My mother said
I never should...."

Your coffin seemed so small;
you really took
no carrying at all.

GHOSTS

Back bedroom and the parlour underneath,
fireplace of rough-sawn stone and polished slate,
the part that used to be his cramped farmstead,
is where all this takes place. Wood-burning stove
is never lit, so there's no tendency
to linger there; year-long you feel the chill.
The kitchen is the space she likes to dwell,
framed by the hearthside's gilding under-glow.
Next door he taps his pipe against the grate,
refills, strikes up. She smells tobacco, hears
his old man's cough-and-hack into the grate,
the chatter of hobnail on flag, discerns
his little dog scrape by into the hall.
Each morning she puts food out for the birds,
nest-boxes everywhere, garden and wood.
She leaves her husband once: "Plenty of time,"
yet when they try, no luck! The only one
she carries through to term is damaged goods,
conceives her canker as a punishment.
Some nights, the cradle ticking like a faint
heartbeat, a live time bomb inside her head,
she hears the cello. Locals tell he played
slow airs when beasts came near their time or yields
were low. The place was blessed with life; kids thrived,
pitched in amongst the calves and lambs, way back.
Half dressed, she conjures him, deep voice, in welsh,
severe. Strong arms wrap round her waist; rough hands
expose her belly, breasts, between her thighs,
as though examining a troubled ewe.
"What are you doing here? Why have you come?"

Peter Branson

WHATEVER HAPPENED TO WILLIAM?

"It's William Bear." Deadpan:
"Best take a look." She read the signs:
an ambulance arrived
to whisk him off and all the way
he moaned, at six weeks old
found flaccid in his cot,
emitting muted, high-pitched fiddle-tones,
the cri du chat.
Stayed touch and go for days.
A copper, in Crown Court
he got away with it -
and she gave him the benefit.

You couldn't take it in. You'd help,
agreed with social services
to mother him while things
got sorted out. Three hours most days,
all supervised, your sister trawled
cold spite into your home,
fouling the atmosphere.
Stone not-quite-dead
that addled cuckoo's egg:
soured thoughts are handcuffed safe
inside a box on which you've scrawled
a 'Do not open' sign.

Guilt churned them in its mauling grip.
The trust invested penned
her fast until she heard
she'd not get William back
while he lived in. That's when she snapped,
fast-forwarded, moved on.
Dark stuff came out:
first wife bludgeoned, off beat;
lost bouts of anger management;
he'd shook the kid, he claimed,
in panic when it fell into a fit –
green fractures partly healed.

Magicians pulled white rabbits from the hat,
staunched tidal bleeds,
brain more or less intact;
lacked powers to conjure back his sight.
Now eight, rage maps
his father's direful fingerprint;
a hobbled horse locked in
his rocking stall, reined by
deep shadow-lands, perpetual night.
Braille wise beyond
what's healthy for his age, he dreams
in tongues, raps time through palsied feet.

ONE FOR SORROW
"One for sorrow, two for joy ..."
("Magpie": traditional rhyme)
The White Lion, Barthomley, Cheshire

Stiff drink, blue sky, autumn dancing outside,
you don't know what to say to him or how.
Eventually you ask about his kids,
dry ground you think. Face drawn and pale, washed out,
the only colour inked inside the deep
cracks of his parchment brow, you wonder what's
beneath the worn straw hat you've never seen
before, relic of seaside jaunts, you guess.

He chats more freely now, like his old self,
warms up, rails on about the government,
recession, student debt. You're torn, surprised
to find him here, tired duffle coat he filled
for twenty years, so frail, stooped over, like
a wraith; last look at his old haunts perhaps;
this ancient pub, oak-boned, magpie, foot-worn,
honed by four centuries of well-spent lives.

Now as he slips into your past, you map
the future in those ghost fey eyes. The church
bell opposite tells one o' clock. You clock
his patent long progression to the door:
seems to spend ages on one step, hard graft,
as if his shoes are battened to the floor,
each move a distant memory he can't
recall. You've waved goodbye but he's still here.

POEMS 'N' PINTS

This could be any town,
tired old committee room
up narrow jointed stairs.
Blokes brushed with anorak,
women in skirt-wigwams,
each takes a turn, performs
bright work. Rehearse, reprise,
there's not much listening
goes on, just showings off.
This is no common muse
to prick out feelings with,
plant words for everyman:
recession, dole and debt;
Iraq, Afghanistan.
Quaint dusty poetry
on bookshop shelves; should this
grow topical you guess
they'd move on somewhere else:
local theatricals,
folk dancing club, life class.
Sniff teargas on the breeze:
the Christian fundies, keen
to wrest control, press on
their home-to-house attacks.
Armed guards and mines
back up the inner city tide
at flood. This lot don't flinch
as mortar fire takes out
the local library,
oblivious to what
is really happening
outside. Stray bullets chip
the old pub front. Gaga
about the last poem read,
some woman who communed
with this small goose, they leave
things far too late. You find
the fire escape as boots
kick in the door. Up there,
right now, all hell is loose ...

SIXTIES

Breasts ripen, apples in
the sun, "It's no big deal!"
your mantra, flesh engorged.
With God onside
for once, thought warp-
speed, running to stay still,
you ban the bomb,
love Che and Uncle Ho.
The time is free
to party, answers in
the wind, real world on hold.
With love an itch and drugs
the magic carpet ride,
"Anything goes" your thrill,
deep down you know.
The loudest voices rant
for workers' rights
and Vietnam.
See them, in city suits,
a decade down,
product of public school.
You're cursed with hindsight, dire
recession, blue-shift, left
to right. Sixties spent twice,
down-sized, your kids moved on,
stumble towards the light.

MARRIAGE LINES

She would have made
a fine ship's carpenter,
reliable, discreet,
confined for months in clamped
uncompromising stench
on long-haul voyages
to other worlds.

Main task, use eyes,
ears, feel, experience
to monitor
those vital signs,
the slow heartbeat
of breathing hull,
rudder and mast.

Fearful to rock the boat,
she bends before
her demon captain's will,
splicing repairs,
re-caulking planks,
treading sea shells
to stave disaster off.

Gentled but unfulfilled
(No fiction this),
she feigns desire,
feels duty-bound,
submission, flattery,
respect. So who are you
to criticise?

E EQUALS M C SQUARED
For June and Drew

Woman in black
comes to your bed again,
all skin and bone astride
your old line-prop.
Down worm-holed tumbling stairs,
she's melted air,
sheets strewn across the turf
like nursery rime.
You think to find
your mother helping out;
it's what she does.
Yet nobody is there:
no father ruminates
at his shed bench, fag-bound;
his father, of the handlebar
moustache, waistcoat
and rolled-up newspaper,
off to the outside lav;
first grandmother,
white as the washing line,
down third year eyes;
the others, dog-ear blurs
on photographs;
no friends, those two who leave
before their span,
he, far too big for everyday
and she, so full of humankind;
no characters;
no fallen heroes, footballers,
outlaws; no freedom fighters, song
birds, writers, poets; the sky
dark matter, empty, fathomless.

LIFE CLASS

Stray girl of eight plays dead, defers her life
for several years, alone, out-blitzed. C.D.
that's snagging on track one, each time you start
her off again she fails at the same spot.
Eventually she shakes herself from sleep
to carry on, changed irredeemably
from who she was to what she has become.
A long term member of her writing group
yet each September she begins afresh,
same train and station, page or two, full stop.
Blacked out, weird sirens like banshees, strange stars
appear between clear pools of fierce moonlight,
as shell fire shakes the shadow-lands beneath.
It starts at Stafford stepping from the train,
name tagged, evacuee down from the Smoke.
Eventually, about six paragraphs,
she joins a family she can't make out
at all near Stoke. That's where her story sticks.
The ravaged sky splits open like pie crust
and she dives in. Bad memories are cut
and spliced, words inked, till there's mere shrapnel left,
the residue of unrequited dreams
she can't construe. Deep in her seventies,
stalled in the Potteries, she's in the groove
again, takes tea and coffee, washes up,
enjoys the gossip of this gang of friends.
What happens to her after she lands here
she finds impossible to call to mind.
Would it be better, do you think, or worse
than old B pictures we have conjured with:
official telegram; footfall outside
her room at night, door slowly opening ...

THE BARTHOMLEY MASSACRE
Near Haslington, South Cheshire

Fresh from an argument with friends, *"That sort
of thing could never happen here,"* a sign
glides by, headlines the total loss at one
black spot in three short years. On Slaughter Hill
you wince inside. A Chinese whispers thing:
"Sloe Tree"? Far-fetched you think, as cavaliers
turn up to cleanse the place of parliament,
high Christmastide of 1643.

This day the Valley Brook is flush with blood.
Some flee to Barthomley, claim sanctuary
inside their parish church, till they are forced
from safety when the tower is put to flame.
*"Twelve men were slaughtered while one youth, his throat
sliced open, bleeds to death before my eyes.
Sweet Jesus Christ!"* Four wounded, three escape
this Calvary of fruitless sacrifice.

KITE FLYING

A kite sails, gracefully, against the breeze,
turning the mountains' pages east to west
along the ridge, this bobby-dazzler day
of bracing cold and blinding light, blue sky
with whispers of sheer white to harmonize.
Your x ray breath is mute and shadow-less,
just like the snow you print frail mantras on
in brail footfalls that all will turn out right.
This walk out in the hills is tiring you -
more than it used to do. The poison pen's
been written; you're still upright though half done.
The kite is consummate in its design,
unlike the one that you've been forced to fly.
You're fathomless; could stall at any time.

ENDGAMES
"Four and twenty blackbirds baked in a pie"
From 'Sing a song of sixpence' (traditional rhyme)

1.
Parliament of Rooks

Conceive a ring of black birds in a field;
an act of faith, like UFOs or ghosts.
Inside this henge, three prisoners face trial,
mid winter, dusk - his story, sold to buy
your proxy vote - fear in their gaze, doom in
their stance; gothic, apocryphal, remote.
When he returns the circle's broken up.
Seduced to take a closer look, he finds
feather haloes; corpses, blinded, half plucked.
Brings back Big Brother love, the guillotine,
stoning to death, neighbourhood bullying
in public view, a signal to the rest,
the righteous punishment for breaking some
unspeakable sectarian taboo.

2.
Rook Sacrifice

Strange now the birds have gone. They came to look
as usual, a day or two, first time
in memory moved on. Last season's nests,
threadbare, holes you can peer straight through, break up
beneath grey skies, abandoned, unredeemed.
The trees are not at risk, from rot, disease,
old age; sound for another century
at least. Place hasn't changed at all and yet ...
These church bells have no competition now.
Just one fresh grave, that murder first house down
the lane; in all the newspapers for days.
South aisle, tall tales are broadcast via stained glass
of superheroes, like in comic books.
Some swear rooks sense a place is tainted, leave.

'HIGH HO SILVER, AWAY!'

1.

Light slides down reels
of spinning celluloid,
freewheels through silvered streams
of space and time where ghosts
dance out from two dimensions, black
on white, rides technicolor myths
to flood the screen.
The stranger in the mask
would choke injustice in a cloud
of dust on sets of cardboard rocks
and plywood frontages,
where punches pull
and shell blanks ricochet.
A cowboy arms and head,
mad galloping
through hobbled streets
on hop-along back legs
and slapping thighs, you'd wing
hostile young kids with finger guns
beneath dark cobbler skies.

2.

That hero tucked inside
your head, recall
first rueful day your thoughts
outgrew his dreams.
He'd conjure reds from greys
where Pax Americana rules,
seal hearts and minds,
Korea, Vietnam,
time-warp, same script,
like Superman and Captain Kirk.
You've seen what's happening:
talking forked tongues in cheek,
('The national interest');
Afghanistan, Iraq; lost souls
in orange isolation suits;
wetbacks who hold
this brave new world intact?
As troops clean up another street,
stars fizzle out, stripes cringe
from sheer embarrassment.

Peter Branson

SHADOW DANCERS

1.
The Swift
Radford Street, Stone, Staffs

Not here this year, lost souls, homes worn away,
handhold to fingertips, like spent pueblos.
They don't die back or hibernate, but cruise
vast distances above the turning world.
July evenings, they side-step, scissor-kick
thin air, etch pen 'n' ink invisible
tattoos. Banshees, dust devils in wet suits,
anchors on skeins of rising light, they're soon
shrill specks in your mind's eye. Time lords, stealth craft
hot wired to while away brief summer nights,
they preen, breed on the wing, use what the wind
blows in to feed, fix nests under house eaves.
Broadcast, they silhouette the urban sky,
shape-shift, in one heartbeat, present and past.

2.
The Hobby
Doxy Marshes, Stafford

Late August daylight crumbles into dust,
the cemetery behind, the marsh ahead;
above, in feeding mode, vast teeming shoals
of double sickle-shapes in silhouette.
One shadow dancer's larger than the rest,
a lithe stealth-jet slip-streaming nimble shrill
spitfires. This deadly symbiotic dance
of insect, swift and falcon must reprise
at watering holes both here and Africa,
points in between, throughout the turning year.
A random pick, or wilful choice perhaps,
within a blink this conjuror can craft
a fallen angel broken on the rack,
a rag doll from a tumbling acrobat.

THE CURLEW
(The curlew is on the red list of species judged to be on the road to extinction.)
"O curlew, cry no more in the air" (W. B. Yeats)

The Peak District National Park

This tearful horn-anglais refrain haunts like
old Irish pipes, high-bubbling trills as shrill
as tribal widowhood. St Beino blessed,
his sermons rescued from the waves, tale goes,
blurred like a needle's eye by candlelight
and lost again before you know, they weave
between two worlds, of living and of dead.
These browns, burnt olives, duns add clout: hard times
abound, present and past; echoes of fly-
blown gunnels and consumptive back to backs;
of guttersnipe, folk old before their span –
famine, disease, debilitating dust;
of gamekeeper, mill owner, magistrate,
pawnbroker, rent collector, tallyman.

Peter Branson

'RAINDROPS KEEP FALLING ON MY HEAD'
Mr & Mrs Harry Place & James Ryan
(Coney Island, New York, February, 1901)

Just as the door to Mr Place's room
begins to close, you glimpse a pistol in
its holster, sort of thing they use out West.
But mindful of his tip, you think no more
of it, until a few days' later, when
you read how Pinkertons have chanced upon
a photograph of members of the Wild
Bunch outlaw gang. And there he is, him with
the classy broad in tow, the Sundance Kid
no less. You recognise the piercing eyes
from the adjacent suite, Butch Cassidy,
would you believe? You dine on him for weeks.
They leave next day, the Argentine, some say.
Whatever, they are never seen again.

"SOME BLESSED HOPE"
New Year, 2012/13

Three quarter century's neglect has left
this feral coppice tired and overspent.
The gate I lean against this blear-eyed New
Year's Day is propped by barbs of rusted wire,
millennium twelve years away, your time
one hundred more, same tune, a sepia ghost.

Fearless, all frost and fire, the stormcock's back,
lights up the swaying oak's exposed topmast;
first salvo, flings its raking challenge in
machine-gun rote, defiant, unabashed,
then charms the darkling treescape with its theme-
song, wassail, band-of-hope – all this despite

the corrugated ground, a spectral, iron
death-mask; our threadbare hospitals and roads;
the central heating on back home full blast;
e money flooding from rogue credit cards
like blood flushed from cadavered-marble slabs;
soldiers in coffins flown from far off lands.

Peter Branson

COMIC CUTS BIN LADEN

'Comic Cuts' was a British amalgam of reprints from US magazines. Hugh Lupus, or Hugh the Wolf, was granted most of Cheshire by his brother in law, William 1. "Killing a captive who poses no immediate threat is a crime." Benjamin Ferencz, a prosecutor at Nuremburg.)

Himself again, pub window seat, tells how
he got laid out upon the bridle-path
behind. A wild beast bars his route. His mount
rears up and that's the last he can recall
until he comes to here, this roadhouse inn,
listed, survivor from the golden age,
white render, Norfolk thatch, for those who could
afford a car way back. Oak panels, beams,
stone inglenook, tall story in stained glass,
fag end Pre-Raphaelite – kills wolf and spares
King John; saves Magna Carta too, drunk with
hindsight. Truth's washed, teased out, spun, woven, cloak
of many hues. It's Pax America
these days; "Geronimo!" Cue Marvelman.

The Bleeding Wolf Inn, circa 1933,
Scholar Green, South Cheshire, 7ᵗʰ May, 2011.

THE BOAT HOUSE
London Rowing Club, Putney

To Chris and Sharon with love

This is the season for it, not when fields
are iced iron-rut or frayed brown corduroy
or loud with corn; rather when bells are pitched
to tune with living things, the rising sap,
white blossom, throstle, lark, hormonal rooks.
These days the stallion's bolted, door distressed -
I'm speaking generally of course – and yet
it's not died out nor been replaced. Young folk
don't change that much, still feel the need to pledge
their truth in front of family and friends,
the world to judge. So what of this bright pair
who've pulled us here today, twin oars - one boat?
They've chosen well I think, each other, this,
the food and drink, the company, the view.

FOUND

*'Rise up, O Lord. May thy enemies be scattered and those who hate thee be
driven from thy face.' (Inscription found on a fragmented strip of gold).
Valuation came in at £3,285,000.*

The Staffordshire Hoard

That high-pitched wail
kicks in, heralds pay-dirt.
The shroud of soil
removed, it surfaces,
loud as a smile above
an open grave;
furrows of gold,
a perfectly-preserved
stillbirth, exposed,
keening and buttery,
just as interred. The field's
been ploughed way back
where this was found,
our Dark Age past exhumed,
torn from the dead.
Was it rough politics,
a secret stash? The cross
was mangled; whiff
of sacrilege, bad blood,
knight sacrifice,
crude tit for tat;
ill fortune best left in
the ground beneath
the dowser's measured feet?
He cried for help.
Light danced before his eyes
in shovel-loads.
Someone was listening.

CROW BAIT

This huge black bird appears from nowhere, prints
its shadow on the lawn beneath your feet.
You're at the washing line, just hanging out,
an ink-blot copy of a winding sheet.
He stands there, unperturbed, three yards away,
beak threatening, knife blade of sharpened flint
staring you in the face, eyes deep as jet.
Later you bring him back to mind, recall
he's gone before you've time to fret, invite
the darkness in. That evening, lights on, home
alone, you shiver, stoke the fire. Afraid
there's dancing over someone's grave, you groan,
brood on your carrion crow, what this might bode -
a hungry door, late night, wild banshee phone?

ONE STEP AWAY
*"In memory of Ephraim Brocklhurst, killed
at Magpie Mine, Jan 20th, 1860, aged 25 yrs.
'There is one step between me and death.'"*
                    (Plaque at Magpie Mine, Sheldon, Derbyshire.)

Autumn, late afternoon; the larks have long
since flung this season's last grace notes sky high.
It's more ruined bailey than abandoned mine
viewed from afar, tall chimneypiece a tower
where maidens were confined till rescued by
some gallant knight, broadsword, blond hair, blue eyed.
A Newcomen made all things possible,
limestone, like linen on the washing line,
dry bones, here alchemists spun lead to gold,
God's will, supplied demand. Outlandish place,
the curlew's tearful dirge their death lament,
like women wailing by an open grave,
those killed, by rote, when rivals smoked them out,
or cursed by widows' mite, still haunt this ground.

THE BIG PICTURE

Way back, after the B film, interlude
(cue sex, uncomplicated stuff, the eye
and such, 'It's Now or Never' land, 'Be Mine
Tonight,' ice cream), lights fade, big picture floods
the screen. This is the country of the blind
where those who see are damned. When ignorance
is bliss, "Consume" the prayer on every lip,
banks bring us to our knees and get away
with it. Debit and credit cards fired from
the hip, the ones with most to lose aren't fazed.
Small fry do time; the poor get sacrificed.
Where trees are camouflage, romantic views
the rage, Art prostitutes itself and paints
its face. The contradictions spread like weeds.

RED STREET

That youngster who is me at primary school
loves Miss to talk-up Empire, half the globe
pale pink. We call it "Commonwealth" and get
on famously, big family, Queen head;
good parent, loyal, caring, fair but tough.
No mention of Korea, massacres
in Kenya and Malaya, news airbrushed,
gunboat diplomacy, torture, dark stuff.

Recall what Ron gets up to in the bogs?
One knuckle duster blow's more than enough,
the rest slow-motion stuff, his prey half-drowned
in piss and blood and all because this lad
is giving his new girl a fleeting look.
Steel toe cap in the ribs and he's long gone,
next day-joined up. That's Ronnie at the bar,
slap head, beer belly, shrunk, forty years on.

RETROSPECT

In Breughel's masterpiece, Joseph and spouse
arrive at Bethlehem to pay their dues,
no hint, before celebrity kicks in,
they're more significant than other folk
out there, soused by the snow. This makes no sense
in geography nor when bowled over by
two thousand years' remorseless spin. Point is
it's what he liked to do – and understood.

Those who knew Newton as a problem child,
had they an inkling what he'd grow to do?
Could smug contemporaries at Eton sense
the Orwell rising in young Eric Blair?
All things are possible. In later years,
no doubt, drunk with hindsight, they drown in clues.

THE FLAX BOW
A tradition of the Cherokee Nation

The squall you sensed tonight would bring has built
into a storm. When latches rattle like
long-dry Morse bones and windows re-invent
themselves, moulding continuously before
your eyes, melting, like ancient 45s,
dark energy you've sacrificed to fire,
each agonising flinch a cruel death mask,
you crave the sanctuary of calm outside.
If you could craft a bow of flax, the roof
green willow sprigs, which bend like compromise,
thread beads, rose quartz for harmony, turquoise
for trust and kindness, amethyst and mother
of pearl, stability, on strings you weave
together, seal with tears like ambergris ...

MUMMY'S BOY

These days, the widow's mite, a perfect son:
no dirty clothing, tissues, mugs and plates
laid down to clutter up his room, lad rags;
no bother at the school – "out of control!"
or with the police, "Glue sniffing", "Theft", "Assault";
no flying furniture or angry doors;
no mad binge drinking, pills, gang fights. Best thing
that ever happened, changed him overnight.

It's all on show: iconic photographs;
Dress uniform, fresh pressed, back of the door;
"Day the whole town turned out" the headline news.
In pride of place, with words like "bravery,
freedom, duty beyond the call, hard blow",
handwritten letter, framed, from his CO.

RODE PARK
Odd Rode Cricket Ground, October, 2011

Rode Park at dusk, fixed as a paragraph,
until, silent as thought, the sparrowhawk
scythes by, well nigh invisible, stage right.
She banks to turn, a living hologram,
pale underbelly harvesting those late
stray stooks of light, reflect cricket off-white,
like dusty porcelain at knock-out price.
Throws up a startled dove, this paraclete,
mad beatings of the air like bongo drums
ignored. No sophistry, she kills to stay
alive; no choice; she's gorged, simple as that;
no fool, no stomach for malevolence,
no psychopath; no bullet in the brain,
revenger's tragedy, bedlam, mob rule.

SPIN

You're live at dawn: highlight the dove, wide screen,
the curtains drawn; snow-white, incongruent
against the sward. He's let them out again,
nine houses up the lane, to pinch the seed
you laid down yesterday. Just when you're set
to raise the roof in angry semaphore,
the picture's razor-sliced from left to right.
Tired synapses kick in, surprise attack:
the sparrow hawk, punching above his weight
this time, turns sideways on to take short shrift,
where feathers harboured vital pulsing flesh
split second back. No space at all, your patch
re-civilised, you watch the thrush, cock-eyed,
as if it's ear-wigging, hair-trigger primed.

Peter Branson

BALLAD OF STEPHEN LAWRENCE
For Stephen Lawrence, 1974 - 1993

Remember Stephen Lawrence?
In April, Ninety-three,
Got set on by a gang of youths
Who robbed his life away.

They left him badly wounded
And bleeding to his death;
As though nothing had happened,
Just hailed a bus and left.

One person who was passing,
Who witnessed the attack:
"They're giving him a kicking
Because his skin is black."

Folk watching had no notion
That he'd been stabbed at all,
But then they watched him stagger,
Fall slowly to the floor.

And even when this happened,
They never understood
A teenager was dying,
Until they saw the blood.

They held his hand in comfort,
Well meaning prayers were said.
Too soon it was all over,
This bright young man was dead.

Though people know who did it,
These thugs got off scot-free,
No murderers found guilty,
Cry foul, conspiracy!

Whole generation later,
It's plain for all to see,
Though two stand new convicted,
Three killers still walk free.

THE CLASS WAR
For Emma

"I don't want to be in this fucking poem!"
is what got said. You black the doorway, bruise
her in your head. Stay calm. Don't show she's got
to you; smile back. Her exit spent, cue for
downstage dumb insolence, barbed-wire backchat
just underneath her breath, yet proud enough
for you to know this isn't any place
you want to go. Drilled since a little kid
she'd make a teenager one day, the price,
see-sawing, self regard now self disgust,
she sneaps you daggered looks. "Yeh, yeh, life sucks!"
is your fined thought, but what's to do if not
to be dishonoured and outfought? Hidebound
by holy ground, hormonal flux, them - us
you can't control nor understand that much,
rub bottom lip, flick index finger down
then back, "Bwub! Bwub!" Sensing an armistice
she feints a flank attack, then suddenly,
hard face caves in, divest all artifice
(disarming), one euphoric gormless grin.

Peter Branson

DOG SOLDIERS

The Dog Soldiers or Dog Men (Cheyenne Hotamétaneo'o) was one of six military societies of the Cheyenne Indians. Beginning in the late 1830s, this society played a dominant role in Cheyenne resistance to American expansion in Kansas, Nebraska , Colorado and Wyoming. Today the Dog Soldiers society is making a comeback in such areas as the Northern Cheyenne Indian Reservation in Montana and among the Cheyenne and Arapaho Tribes in Oklahoma.

We're alpha male, war-paint, full battle dress,
ride ponies, single file, careful to write
no message on the flawless parchment sky.
We come and go, werewolves, dust-devils, ghosts,
in shadow-land till spirits cry "It's time!"
Fast in the earth beneath our feet, pinned down
by golden arrows, there's no second way,
hope of retreat. The chiefs talk peace. They know
the Yankees are too powerful to drive
away. Don't take the long term view, world-wise,
missiles and moneybags, oil rights, foresee
the genocide, measles, smallpox and flu,
whisky, mass slaughter of the buffalo.
The Dog Men wait, White Eyes. Our day will come.

THE HADITHA MASSACRE
For Woody Guthrie

Haditha, Iraq, where 14 men, 3 women &
7 children were killed, Nov 24th, 2005.

Come all fair-minded people,
Pray listen to my song,
You police a foreign country,
How things go badly wrong.

Small town down by the river,
No special claim to fame,
Till US troops were ambushed
There; one of them was slain.

A passing car got peppered
Beneath a blazing sun.
Five bodies were recovered
But not one single gun.

They stormed the nearby houses
And heard their sergeant say
"Fire first, ask questions later,"
For someone had to pay.

Bad apples in a barrel,
The warning signs ignored,
Each time we turn a blind eye
Means bigger trouble stored.

Three women, seven children
And fourteen men lay dead.
The youngest still a toddler,
Aged one, the locals said.

It's hard to find excuses
When so much blood was shed.
Yet no one has been punished,
No justice for the dead.

They shot some at close quarters,
A bullet in the brain.
An old man in a wheelchair
Was numbered with those slain.

I don't know why we came here,
I've no idea at all,
'less it's for the money men
Who buy and sell our oil.

HILLSBOROUGH

At the F A Cup semi-final betweenLiverpoolandNottingham Forest on 15th April 1989, overcrowding resulted in the deaths of 96 people with 766 others injured. All were supporters of Liverpool F. C.
(Main melody: 'The Sharpsville Massacre,' by Ewan McColl. Chorus: 'The Rising of the Moon', J C Carey, arr. Luke Kelly)

It's Saturday, so what's the rush,
And why that soppy grin?
I'm on my way to Hillsborough,
The FA Cup to win.
Though road works cause a bottleneck,
We're here for three o'clock.
There's crushing on the terraces;
Two pens are overstocked.

Chorus: You'll never walk alone my friends,
You'll never walk alone.
St James Park to White Hart Lane,
You'll never walk alone.

I ask where all the bobbies are,
Why safety doors are locked.
Some folk round here are dying,
Yet still the match kicks off.
We can't believe what's happening,
Shocked people stand and stare:
The pitch is like a battlefield
with bodies everywhere.

Chorus

It's funeral after funeral,
Seems far too much to bear;
Whole city is united
as anger trumps despair.
Police evidence gets doctored,
It's always been the same;
The great and good colluding,
To their eternal shame.

Chorus

The Sun crawls out one morning
The wrong side of the bed:
Swears fans were drunk and violent
And looted their own dead.
The inquest rules by three-fifteen
All ninety-four had died.
We now know there were forty-one
Who might have been revived.

Chorus

The final toll is ninety-six,
The youngest aged just ten;
One man's four years on life support
But never speaks again.
In twenty-twelve we're told the truth,
What football's always known.
St James' Park to White Hart Lane,
You'll never walk alone.

Chorus

PUB FOLK
The Greyhound, Newcastle

Not in it for the wealth or fame, don't crave
an audience, beyond each other, in
the moment, dancing fingertips a blur.
Small talk is jigs and airs, sour-sweet grace notes,
same tune on fiddle, banjo, mandolin
and flute. Brother and sisterhood, streetwise,
apprentices and artisans, maestros,
they play for pleasure, raise themselves above
the everyday. Their instruments are wild
things, reeling, bucking broncos, bulls with blood-
shot eyes. Each sense alive, at stretch to stay
onside, they seed each other's gaze with smiles.
This is subversive, dangerous, black art;
pure energy, communion of parts.

KINDOKI
For Kristy

Was it because they could, mere whim, this pair
became inquisitors, or was belief
the seed that thrived, instilled the need to drive
out sin with hammer, chisel, metal bar
and pliers? Damned by the truth, damned if they lied,
no squeals of glee, just children terrified.
One sibling swears in evidence, 'I don't
know what was going on inside their minds
for there was nothing we could say to stop
the beatings.' Afterwards they're forced to wash
away their brother's blood. But surely this,
witches and stuff, is ancient history;
outside, England we know, suburb and town,
park, supermarket, restaurant, traffic light?

FOX TOR MIRES
(Geat Grimpen Mire: 'The Hound of the Baskervilles')

Don't lose your grip. Take care when mist slides in,
stick with known paths. Green counterpane palpates,
seductive, soft as eider down beneath
your feet. Alone, both limbs shin-deep in ice-
cold peat, you're ancient mummery, burnt toast.
Up here at night, it's easy to conceive
satanic rites abound, big cats, hellhounds.
We lust for faith, belief in stuff beyond
the ken of science, concede defeat. Way down
inside abandoned shafts and unmapped walk-
ways, ancient mind workings, rogue programs in
the genes go live, sans over-ride, self load.
Ghost virals we can't shake inoculate,
draw out death's sting, shroud darkness in white light.

NARROW-BOATS AT RODE HEATH RISE

Lump hammers clang; before you know, beyond
your spring-soft garden greens, they're in your face,
proud ring a roses livery, war paint,
throat-lozenge shapes, like coffins in a plague.
Slow-time machine, parallax universe,
sterns list where tethered heavy-horses strain;
bows nodding-donkey ride, tease air for sign
of hostiles, like old wagon-trains in films.

It's handy for the all day shop and pub,
next lock. No space to form a circle though;
exposed to locals on the towpath side
who wander by with dogs or fishing looks.
Young bucks on motor bikes who like to make
a splash - disturbing that, take turns nearby.

FOLK RISING
The Packhorse, Longport, Stoke-on-Trent
For Bert Lloyd and Ewan McColl

Ghost music; can you hear – sing rounds in back-
street pubs, circle complete? Back when they thought
the muse was dead, cool workers' kids, released
from grammar school, go dowsing, kiss it back
to life; warm function rooms, God on their side,
to tales of miners, drovers, highwaymen;
subversive undertow, with 'Ban the Bomb!'
and "Uncle Ho,' defiance at flood tide.

It couldn't last. The moguls changed their tune,
signed likely lads, stars in their eyes; folk rock
drowned out the words. Gone underground, down-sized
yet in rude health - until next time, so keep
it to yourself; new songs to tell it like
it is when roused by breach of commonwealth.

Peter Branson

'JUST YOU WAIT AND SEE'
from 'The White Cliffs of Dover' (at Burton/Vera Lynn)

Some species of long-distance spring migrants are declining
in numbers at an accelerating, possibly unsustainable, rate.

Tonight the sky's all pulsing hearts, concealed
like stars beyond the Milky Way. Not shape-
shifters nor sleeping ones the Hopi knew,
half ours, alternative far worse, they chase
the tilt of Earth and charm us with their voice;
heralds, angels on high, the clout inbred,
trade weather, desert, ocean, birds of prey,
for daylight, food, fair chance to breed and thrive.
What if they don't turn up, flycatcher, swift,
warbler and turtle dove, those cuckoos in
'The Times,' that nightingale in Berkeley Square?
Will spring go missing too? Inexorable
high tide; you don't believe it possible?
It's here; get real, bluebirds at 12 O'clock.

SCOUSE JACK
('Scouse': a Liverpool stew)

An inner émigré, he's hard to pin,
urbane, that razor wit, well-honed in youth,
reined back and kindly-used. Rare time when drink
cuts in, just two or three, shield brows relent,
shy scamp again, deep furrows harrowed out.
Salt twang he ditched, when elocution blitzed
at grammar school, returns "Address unknown";
vowels broaden, consonants go walkabout.
Take stock of Saxon, Viking, Norman, Celt,
sea gypsy, refugee, bondman and slave,
scran hostel, hovel, bawdy, drinking dive,
constituents of rabid enterprise,
add spice from Orient and Africa,
rich mix to tease and whet the appetite.

Peter Branson

MISE-EN-SCÈNE

1.
Tomb Effigy, Wells
Large cracks began to appear in the tower structure. In fear of a total collapse, several attempts at internal strengthening and buttressing were made, until the famous 'scissor arches' were put in place by master mason William Joy between 1338 & 1348.

Chased out of rock laid down in salt lagoons,
BC, Old Testament, pre humankind,
before the dinosaurs, you rest here on
your crib of self-indulgences, paid for,
fair copy of what's rotted underneath.
This leprous nose is flattened out, the stone
dissolving, cartilage, bone congealed like wax,
the Silent Scream played on a misericord,
a hard road to salvation twelve-bar blues.
Is it good luck to rub your ghost facade,
a rite to keep believers safe from spells,
the charm of gravity, collapsing walls,
tamed here by master mason's scissor trick,
until the early warning trumpet calls?

2.
Bath Abbey, West Front

Round here, even the scroungers are well-heeled
and know it's not polite to poop on folk
who take their ease at pavement coffee bars,
corralled, led by the credit card. Gulls strut
like troubadours, sleek pigeons dance between
packed chairs and tables, standing legs, tired feet.
Broad cappuccino smiles of customer
and bird alike are matched and mirrored by
milk chocolate swirls, stirred logos of desire.
And from the tall west frontage of the church,
in your mind's eye, God gazes down, benign,
above the scant remains of angels long
since ill defined, and saints with bare-faced flaws,
blunt-nosed, expressionless and disinclined.

3.
Hunter's Moon
Cathedral of St Michael, Coventry, November 14th, 1940

The bulldog breed don't beat retreat, to view
toy town, close weave of hearth and industry,
emblazoned by a quisling Palmer sky.
Berlin gets blitzed, its people terrorised.
These wailing high tsunamis, wave on wave
of fallen angel-fuelled raw spite, are tit
for tat, massed thunderheads and balls of light,
hard raining hell on earth for anti Christ.
A dragon sucking in cold air to feed
itself, the old place glows white hot. New church
is raised, a garden made, the cross of nails,
'Father forgive.' Ruined walls retained, lest we
forget, St Michael drives the devil out,
with God on side for once; from evil good.

4.
The Ladies of the Vale
Lichfield, Staffordshire, July, 2012

It's special here, a time machine, grace notes
we sense but can't explain, quantum good will.
Dark Ladies of the Vale command the view,
in widows' weeds, just like when Parliament
lay siege, the reek of powder on the breeze,
the talk of sorcery and regicide
Pass bunting Jubilee, red, white and blue,
criss-crossing narrowed sky like razor wire.
See saints and angels soar like kittiwakes
west face, three spires severe as witches hats,
space acrobats, defying gravity
on wing and prayer, Inside, all reliquary
defiled, carved heads lack noses, puritan
distaste for ornament, whole site ransacked.

5.
The Spire
Salisbury Cathedral from the Bishop's Grounds
(John Constable, c.1825)

My constant faith to seek out truth first hand,
sketch places I know best for canvasses
nigh on impossible to sell, I'm forced
to take up portraiture to make ends meet.
This painting was commissioned by my friend,
John Fisher. See him with his wife beneath
these elms, the meadows drained, church settled where
the deer gave up the ghost, as legend tells.
There is no easy way to paint a pure
and unaffected scene, movement and light,
for landscape alters as the weather does.
The spire stands tall against the sky, yet here
it's dwarfed and tempered by these ancient trees,
rainbow behind, dark thunderhead on high.

MARILYN
Born Norma Jeane Mortenson; 1926 – '62
(Westwood Memorial Park, Los Angeles)

The flowers turn up, like memories of long-
lost friends, tears of regret, fifty years on.
Whisper wet dream; blue angel eyes, red lips;
sheer gown, spray-on, no panties underneath.
Dumb blond, by product of the casting couch,
lucid, well read; the Magdalene, "Je t'aime!"
"It's happy birthday, Mister President",
Marie Celeste: the contradictions spread.
Say Marilyn, feel love, but is it real?
Think past the fantasy to Norma Jean;
calendar girl found naked on her bed,
the fallen star, barren, burnt out, alone.
It's not unusual, the pills and booze,
Doc Hollywood, dead hand on siren phone.

ESSERE AMATA AMANDO
('To love and to be loved')
Alice Douglas-Pennant, Penrhyn Castle, 1880

I gaze down from my ivied tower room
on lean-to greenhouses and potting sheds,
walled garden where we met, etch words of love
here on this diamond page of leaded glass.
Childhood charmed us invisible, times when
the governess was occupied, young girl
and keeper's son. And nothing changed till you
were old enough to join the outside staff
and I was on the cusp of womanhood.
Eyes and ears everywhere, silent as wraiths,
the housemaids come and go, unseen, between
two worlds, this and the one below the stairs
where gossip brewed. The butler passed it on.
Now I've been banished here and you have gone.

Peter Branson

THE SPIRIT MASK

Before dawn dark, beyond the kissing gate,
no trace of human enterprise, year's edge
and seasonably cold, big moon hoodwinked,
the wood's re-wilding at flood tide. Alone,
anything's possible, hair trigger primed.
You conjure up the company of wolves,
soundscape all eyes. Words come to mind but not
tall stories, shepherds' lore, Red Riding Hood.
Too soon, the darkness draining like a half-
blocked waste, they melt away like smoke. As light
re-civilises things, with nature trained
on gibbet, poison, snare and gun, recall
men in wolf heads, dead outlaws posed by ghosts
of bounty men, snug in your sheepskin coat.

Red Hill